D0860447

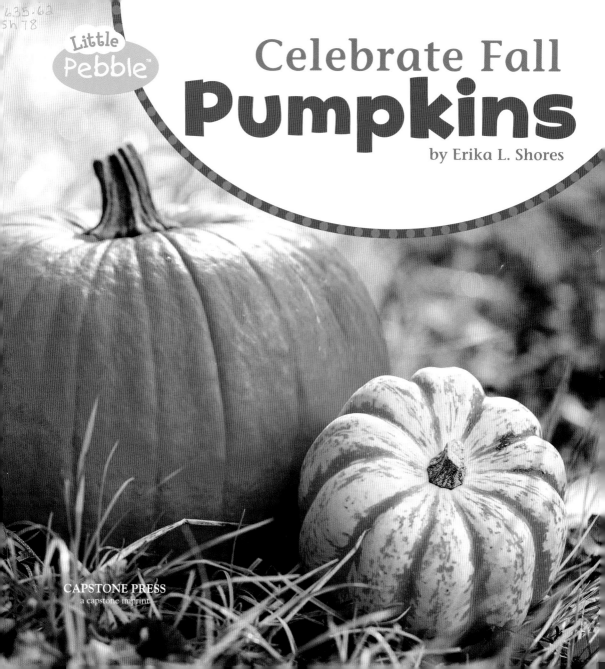

Little
Pebble™

Celebrate Fall
Pumpkins

by Erika L. Shores

CAPSTONE PRESS
a capstone imprint

Little Pebble is published by Capstone Press,
1710 Roe Crest Drive, North Mankato, Minnesota 56003
www.capstonepub.com

Library of Congress Cataloging-in-Publication Data
Shores, Erika L., 1976– author.
 Pumpkins / by Erika L. Shores.
 pages cm.—(Little pebble. Celebrate fall)
 Summary: "Simple nonfiction text and full-color photographs present pumpkins in fall"—Provided by the publisher.
 Audience: Ages 5–7
 Audience: K to grade 3
 Includes bibliographical references and index.
 ISBN 978-1-4914-6004-7 (library binding)—ISBN 978-1-4914-6016-0 (pbk.)
 ISBN 978-1-4914-6028-3 (ebook pdf)
 1. Pumpkin—Juvenile literature. 2. Autumn—Juvenile literature.
 I. Title.
 SB347.S56 2016
 635.62—dc23   2015001837

Editorial Credits
Cynthia Della-Rovere, designer; Gina Kammer and Morgan Walters, media researchers; Katy LaVigne, production specialist

Photo Credits
Capstone Studio: Karon Dubke, 13, 15, 19; Dreamstime: Radzian, 5; iStockphoto: Renphoto, 21; Shutterstock: Alena Brozova, (sequence growing plant) backcover, Dancake, (dots on border) throughtout , Denis and Yulia Pogostins, 17, Earl D. Walker, 11, fuyu liu, (green vine) throughout , Kim Reinick, 20, Leigh Prather, (fresh pumpkin) 3, 24, marisc, 1, mikeledray, 6, 7, 9, MountainHardcore, cover

Printed in China
032015   008832LEOF15

Table of Contents

In the Fall

The weather turns cool.

It is fall.

Look at the pumpkins!

They grow in a patch.

Pumpkins grow
on vines along
the ground.

vine

8

Grab pumpkins
by the stems.
Pile them into carts.

stem

Seeds

Cut into a pumpkin.

Take out the 200 seeds.

12

13

Seeds are sticky.

Save them.

Plant them in spring!

The sun shines.

Rain falls.

Watch the seeds sprout.

Vines grow.
Pumpkins get bigger.

Time to pick

the perfect one!

Glossary

patch—a small part or area

seed—the part that will grow into a new plant

sprout—to start to grow

stem—the part of a plant that connects the roots to the leaves

vine—a plant with a long thin stem that grows along the ground or up a fence

Read More

Felix, Rebecca. *We Harvest Pumpkins in the Fall.* Let's Look at Fall. Ann Arbor, Mich.: Cherry Lake Pub., 2013.

Griswold, Cliff. *The Pumpkin Patch.* Fun in Fall. New York: Gareth Stevens Publishing, 2015.

Smith, Sian. *What Can You See in Fall?* Seasons. Chicago: Capstone Heinemann Library, 2015.

Internet Sites

FactHound offers a safe, fun way to find Internet sites related to this book. All of the sites on FactHound have been researched by our staff.

Here's all you do:
Visit *www.facthound.com*
Type in this code: 9781491460047

Super-cool stuff!

Check out projects, games and lots more at
www.capstonekids.com

Index